SANCT

Finding a New Relationship with the Land

by Elisabeth Edwards, Fionnuala O'Hare
Kath Simmonds, Jill Taylor & Sue Weaver
with illustrations by Tamaris Taylor

A Simple Living Series Book

Published in the UK by:
Permanent Publications
Hyden House Limited, The Sustainability Centre, East Meon, Hampshire GU32 1HR
Tel: 01730 823 311
Fax: 01730 823 322
Overseas: (int. code +44 1730)
Email: info@permaculture.co.uk
Web: www.permaculture.co.uk

US distributors:
Chelsea Green Publishing Company
PO Box 428, White River Junction, VT 05001
Tel: 802 295 6300
Fax: 802 295 6444
Web: www.chelseagreen.com

First published 2002

Designed and typeset by John Adams

Printed by Antony Rowe Ltd, Chippenham, Wiltshire.

Printed on Elemental Chlorine Free (ECF) paper

British Library Cataloguing-in-Publication Data.
A catalogue record for this book is available from the British Library.

ISBN 1 85623 020 1

The Authors

Elisabeth Edwards lives in Cardiff, in a small terraced house with a tiny walled garden which is damp, shady, an ideal home for slugs and snails. She is passionate about insects and all the tiny life forms which are so often overlooked. After years of trying to grow 'garden' plants she heard the call for a native tree, and planted a hawthorn. House sparrows and many other small birds came to feed in its branches, and swifts to feed on the insects in the sky above. As she has watched the tree and the garden change and grow through the seasons she has learned awareness of the great cycles of the Earth. She's learned, too, that this land expresses itself most beautifully in the subtle greens of damp woodland, rich with ferns, mosses and ivies.

Fionnuala O'Hare returned to Ireland, the land of her birth, in 1997, after many years living in London, and moved from a flat with a roof terrace of window-boxes to a small stone cottage with a one-acre field in the Sligo countryside. After securing the land with fencing and planting hedgerows of native trees, she has let it rest and slowly tell her what to do next. Mostly the land wants to be still, sometimes there are suggestions – a pond here, native hardwood or fruit trees there, feeding stations for the birds in the far corner. From her land Fionnuala can see Keash cairn and link to the ancient hills of Knocknarea and Benbulbin, and all the while feel the gradual meeting of human with the Earth.

Kath Simmonds moved from London to Wales in 1975, to a smallholding near Lampeter, with goats, horses, poultry and a large vegetable garden. In 1981 she bought fifteen acres of rough farmland and river valley in mid-Wales, with the dream of restoring the land to a place of sanctuary for native plants and animals. Her experiences in doing this provide much of the practical advice given in this book. Through hard work, always inspired by listening to this beautiful land, her dream has become reality, a home and a haven rich in plants and birds. Kath works as an acupuncturist to support herself, spending weekends and odd days on such things as hedgelaying, tree thinning, fence repairs and gardening.

Jill Taylor lives with her partner, two dogs, a cat, hens, two Gloucester cows and two small flocks of Welsh Badger-faced and Soay sheep on a ten-acre smallholding in the former South Wales coalfield. The land is high and exposed, with a public lane running across it. It's part rough grazing, part woodland, part bog, and twenty years ago was overgrazed and depressed. By hedging, fencing, planting trees and reducing the number of grazing animals the heart and vitality have gradually returned to the land. Now the wood is full of bluebells and nesting birds, new species of wildflowers appear each year and the wild secret places have re-established themselves. On a clear night the land reaches out into the vastness of the open sky above it. Living here has been a journey of discovery for Jill, and she has grown into an entirely different relationship with the animals, the land and its unseen guardians.

Sue Weaver moved in 1999 from a Northamptonshire garden to a seventy-three acre farm in West Wales, with unimproved wet grassland, flower meadows and ancient woodland. Neighbours' cattle graze the land in summer to help preserve the rich meadow flora, and she has learnt about fencing to keep them out of the woods. Hedges, ditches, ponds and woods are slowly teaching her what they need. The farm costs, including one day a week labour, are more than covered by conservation grants and rents. She works part-time as a psychotherapist – when she can tear herself away from deer, red kites, buzzards, otters and badgers.

SANCTUARY

This book is dedicated to Grandmother Earth
and all her guardians

Preface

We started to write this book in the autumn of 2000, and it was almost complete in February 2001 when foot-and-mouth disease began to spread through Britain's countryside. What happened during the months that followed was a nightmare for everyone who cares about the land. Those of us with livestock stayed in virtual isolation, and all of us felt strongly that this was a time for the land to be free from human interference. This book, too, lay fallow during that time, as our energies went into praying for those affected, human, animal and land. Now that we have returned to and completed the book, its message of encouragement and advice for people wishing to hold parts of the Earth as sanctuary has taken on a new urgency – while the removal of so many grazing animals may prove to have been a welcome rest for parts of the land, the toxic effects of the countless gallons of disinfectant which entered our watercourses during those months will last for decades. Yet there are also new openings for change, and a growing awareness among policy-makers and farmers of the destructive effects of intensive farming. Those who are able to hear the voice of the land and to stand as guardians are needed now as much as ever.

May 2002

Contents

Introduction

This book is about a new – and very ancient – way of relating to land, to wherever on this Earth we have chosen to live. It is for people who want to find a different way of being with their land, whatever its size.

We, the writers, have a variety of experiences to offer: between us we hold land as refuge for native plants and animals, as smallholding with livestock, as conservation area, as urban garden. This book has come into being as a result of the questions we have been asking about how to be with our places on the land, as humans who wish to live in harmony with our environment.

We believe that it is vital to find a way to be with the Earth which is not human-centred. This starts from trying to be aware of the voice of the Earth herself, and then being guided by what we hear. In doing this we become guardians of parts of the Earth, which we hold as sanctuary. It is a living, constantly-evolving process, and one we wish to share with you in these pages, through practical advice, suggestions and ideas.

Guardianship can operate on any scale, from large farm to small garden. It may mean giving an over-grazed field the opportunity to recover its once-rich flora and fauna, caring for a particular tree, or simply spending time with plants in a different way. For one person it may mean setting some of their land aside, entirely free from human contact – for another it may be about farming or gardening with a new awareness. If you have no land in your personal care, you can stand as guardian for an area of public land, for a wood or park or beach. Every part of the Earth held as sanctuary will be unique, the living result of a loving relationship between human and land.

"*This we know; the Earth does not belong to humanity; people belong to the Earth, this we know. All things are connected. Whatever befalls the Earth, befalls the people of the Earth. We do not weave the web of life, we are merely a part of it. Whatever we do to the web, we do to ourselves.*" Chief Seattle

The Story of a Welsh Sanctuary

For more than two decades Kath Simmonds has been the guardian of an area of hillside and woodland in West Wales, formerly grazed by sheep, now rich in species.

In 1981 I bought a range of farm buildings and about fifteen acres of land on a hillside in the Teifi Valley, in mid-Wales. This included about three acres of quite good agricultural land, about seven acres of rather boggy rough pasture, and a few acres of wooded river valley. In 1988 I surrounded the land with a sheep-proof fence, and since then it has been grazed only by three ponies. I planted some 3,000 mixed native deciduous trees on the rough pasture, and after about seven years tree-pipits moved in there to nest – declaring it a wood, I felt.

One field of the 'quite good agricultural land' is managed by having hay taken from it each year, since it is now classified as 'unimproved meadow' and is very rare. Taking hay off it ensures that it keeps its exquisitely beautiful variety of flowering plants. When I moved here, it was indistinguishable from the rest of the valley – but since then every field for a long way around has been 'improved' into a green desert of ryegrass, sheep and crows.

This land now supports a wide variety of thrushes, warblers and other birds, including many that are decreasing at an alarming rate elsewhere, such as spotted flycatchers and song thrushes. Some of these were present in small numbers when I came here, and have increased in number dramatically since sheep were excluded, but others have arrived since then (such as woodcock, blackcap, garden warbler, siskin and twite).

I bought this land to provide a wildlife haven because our native habitats are disappearing so fast. Perhaps only a generation ago the farmland of Wales was a delight of wildlife. Walking across a patch of rough grazing one would see flowers, insects, birds in profusion – and this in every valley, not just in the occasional remnant which somebody has preserved, as now. Linnets, yellowhammers, stonechats, orchids, weasels – all these may still be seen in Wales, but only as an occasional glimpse in 'special' places, no longer in every other field. In the uplands, sheep were everywhere, as now, but in drastically smaller numbers, so there were also heather, skylarks, meadow pipits, wheatears, grouse, short-eared owls, golden plover and many other species, which again are now rarities.

This decline stems from changes in farming practices, brought about largely because of the European Union's Common Agricultural Policy (CAP) and its subsidy system, which rewards farmers for overstocking, overgrazing and for so-called 'improving' grassland – by ploughing up meadow and pastureland rich in flowers and insects, draining boggy patches (which support a wide variety of wildlife, from cottongrass and sundew to snipe and newts) and planting monoculture ryegrass.

The end results are what now makes up most of the landscape of Wales and other upland areas of the UK: 'green deserts' of 'improved' grassland, with sheep, crows, buzzards, and very little else – a few magpies and wood pigeons, but no small birds, no undergrowth, no flowers, very little insect life and no birdsong.

More people are now realising what has been done to the landscape of these islands in the race to produce the 'food mountains' that cause such headaches for the EU, and in the name of cheap food for all. Reform of the CAP is beginning to happen, but exactly what the effects will be is as yet unknown. Farming in general is suffering huge financial losses, and was devastated by the slaughter of millions of animals during the foot-and-mouth crisis of 2001. It is understandable that most farmers are concerned more with their immediate financial survival than with the ancient tradition of passing the land on in good heart, as a living, balanced ecosystem that is sustainable indefinitely without the massive input of artificial chemicals.

Under the old traditional ways of farming, the uplands of the UK supported maybe a third of the number of sheep they hold today, while the mixed vegetation grazed by the animals kept them comparatively healthy. The huge expansion in the numbers of sheep has had disastrous consequences. The hillsides are now covered with monoculture ryegrass, planted to support all these animals, its growth artificially stimulated with chemical fertiliser. Overstocking is the norm, but keeping sheep in high densities on this limited diet produces unhealthy animals, with little resistance to infection and parasites. They need constant dosing with chemicals, some of which, like the organo-phosphates in sheep-dip, are extremely toxic. Such chemicals are very damaging to the ecosystem – for example, some wormers used on livestock kill dung beetles, thus interfering with the natural cycle of the breakdown of dung and its return to the soil. Watercourses, too, are frequently polluted by sheep dip and other chemicals, or by fertiliser run-off.

The imbalance between land and livestock has a further effect, which touches all of us, whether we live in city or country. Soil compacted by millions of hooves develops a hard crust, so that water runs off rather than being absorbed by the soil beneath. This is a major cause of the widespread and increasingly frequent flooding of recent years.

Sadly, the intensive approach to food-production predominates, with many farmers continuing to 'improve' their land: bulldozing hedgerows, draining wet areas, spreading fertilisers, pesticides and weedkillers with a heavy hand, and overgrazing the land to within an inch of its life.

So what can be done? There are many possible responses, from indifference, rage and despair to political action, or putting energy into educating the public, particularly the young, to see, understand and appreciate what is happening and how, if we continue, birdsong and wildflowers may be known to future generations only through CDs and videos. The present move towards

organic farming should help things considerably. Any piece of land, large or small, that is not overgrazed, and does not have toxic chemicals applied to it, will help.

Changes in the subsidy system are starting to appear, towards rewarding farmers financially for being more 'environmentally friendly'. These changes are heartening and encouraging for those of us who have been watching the degradation of the countryside with dismay, but they are still in their early stages, and bureaucratic wheels do turn slowly.

The individual response I am called to make is to act as guardian to a piece of land, to allow it to grow and flourish as it would like to be, much as it would have been until quite recently. My hope, and prayer, is that when understanding grows, and policies and farming practices change so that farmland is not so hostile to wildlife, there will be enough species left in sufficient numbers, living in reserves, sanctuaries and similar places, for these to act as reservoirs for the re-population of surrounding farmland with songbirds, wild flowers, insects, small mammals and all the rest.

It is so long now since any of Wales was truly wild that we can only guess what it might have been like. But the farmed landscape that was here until the last few decades had changed little for hundreds of years, and always included a rich variety of wildlife. So when we talk about conservation now, we are usually talking about managing land in such a way as to allow the survival of the species which have been part of the traditional farmed landscape.

Like other upland areas of the UK, most of Wales has been chewed to the ground by sheep. If sheep are excluded from a piece of land for a few years, the transformation is extraordinary, quite magical, as regeneration happens, undergrowth appears, small birds move back in, flowers re-appear, in amazing variety and profusion. As yet, the seeds and occasional chewed remnants of a wide variety of plants must still be surviving on land where little is able to grow because of the devastating overgrazing.

Different ways of managing the land – like grazing, or cutting hay, at different times of the year – affect what wildlife comes to live there. There is no one right way to manage a field or a patch of woodland. There are ways that are clearly destructive, like chemical poisoning or overgrazing, but often there are many different ways, all of them beneficial to wildlife. Sometimes we need to make a choice, which may be to just allow the land to find its own way. For example, a patch of rough grazing kept as lightly-grazed pasture is likely to have an interesting variety of flowering plants in it, and to be good hunting ground for owls and kestrels. Kept ungrazed, it will revert to birch and willow scrub, and become full of all sorts of small birds and different varieties of plants. You may want to keep the brambles down to allow bluebells and knapweed (beloved by butterflies) to flourish, or decide to give the brambles their head, a gift to warblers and other small birds, as well as to many insects and small mammals such as shrews and voles.

In terms of wildlife conservation and helping the land to survive it's hard to go wrong – you don't need to be a wildlife or farming expert. If you simply keep the grazing light, or have none at all, and don't poison the land, you'll be making a wonderful gift to the land and to the future.

The Need for Sanctuary

Somehow we have lost the understanding of the balance of our Earth, of the interrelationship of all life. No longer do we revel in the diversity of life, of the soil, the plants and animals. Instead, it is routine for most farmers and gardeners to try to kill every living thing seen as a possible threat to a bumper crop, or a lawn like a snooker-table. We destroy animals and plants which we label 'wildlife', forgetting that they are vital for the existence of our planet. So we are at war with life itself, and in the process we are slowly, but surely, destroying our Earth.

"*In 50 years the US has, with intensive pesticide use, doubled the amount of crops lost to pests.*" Jules Pretty, The Living Land

In seeking to banish and control the wild we turn our backs on the rich ferment of creation itself, of diversity and abundance. Food-production has concentrated on a handful of the 80,000 potentially edible plants in the world, and today a mere thirty crops supply ninety-five per cent of our nutrition. Just eight of these, led by wheat, rice and maize, provide a staggering three-quarters of our diet.

To hold land as sanctuary is to go against this trend. This concept is not new, but nowadays it is unusual. Yet there is a great need for people to learn again a way of living in harmony with the land. This is becoming obvious as we see the effects of more than half a century of industrial-scale agriculture here in these small islands, and the global effects of human pollution and fossil-fuel use. There is a different way; we can choose to take a guardianship role in order to listen to and support the land and its plants and animals, for the mutual benefit of all, including us. It is the opposite of exploitation; yet it is more than conservation.

It is very difficult for people living in our time and culture to envisage land as being anything other than something from which we gain benefit. We are used to an economic relationship of some kind. Land has a price-tag, and a financial return is expected. Historically the ownership of large tracts of land, whether Cornish fields or Scottish moor, has carried with it power, titles and rights, a system which still profoundly influences the way our society functions. Vast areas of the British countryside are owned by people who may never set foot on their investments, and even conservation land may become a source of revenue, open to the public for a fee.

The most familiar economic use of land is to produce food, and modern farming, of the kind funded and encouraged by governments, requires the land to supply maximum food for maximum profit. From this perspective, it becomes almost a moral imperative to make as much from the land as possible. The growth of organic farming is welcome, with its emphasis on sustainability and the long-term health of the land, but it is still about production and profit. Even small landowners seeking self-sufficiency have to ensure their own survival, putting their own needs above those of the land. They may minimise pollution and human impact, but this is still not the same as the keeping of sanctuary.

To hold land as sanctuary is to enter into a different relationship. People may ask 'But what do you use it for?' to which there is no answer, for it is not about 'use'. This is a co-operative relationship, one of co-creation in which the power relationships and the economics shift dramatically. As people who hold land in this way we can see ourselves as part of a web of interactions, not as the dominant species out to gain control and exploit, but as participants in a natural system.

We are powerful participants: we can dominate, if we so choose, and we must certainly make a lot of decisions, but as participants we can seek to listen to the needs of all the other elements in this complex web of life. And all those other elements can get on perfectly well without us.

Like Any Mother

I'm a lot like you.
I seek fulfilment, joy, bonding,
I too have desires and needs – as you do.
Like any mother I delight in being with my children
and seeing them grow strong;
for I want to see my family excel and live to their full potential.
My children are the rocks, streams, trees and animals, and
like any mother I wail and mourn when they are heartlessly cut down.
I need to feel loved and respected for what I am, not for the riches I have;
though, like any mother, all that I am I freely give my children.
Like any mother, it is the lost child I watch for the most;
and I say to you, human child – find sanctuary in me.
And know, as you create sanctuary for your brothers and sisters,
you also return home to me.

Listening to the Land

When we look at a landscape, we see the shapes of the land, hills and valleys and mountains, shadowed by cloud or lit by sun, clothed with trees and grass, marked with the human signs of fields, buildings and roads. When we look closer, or deepen our awareness further, the generalised green of the plants becomes variety – crops, 'wild' plants – and among them the animals – sheep and cattle, horses, birds, foxes, rabbits, mice, a multitude of insects. And if we send our awareness still further, look more deeply, we begin to see the invisible web connecting all these with the environment around them: sun and rain, wind and air above the ground and, below it, the wonderful variety of rocks and soil and the countless billions of life-forms within the soil, from moles and reptiles to worms, insects, fungi and bacteria.

Practically speaking, what this means is that when we want to co-operate and co-create with land, we need to attend to very many different and not always visible elements: to sun and wind, to water and stream, to rocks and soils beneath, as well as to what we see on the surface, to trees, grasses and animals. Thinking about land in this way means everything we do has meaning – how we heat our houses, where our waste water goes, where we get our water from in the first place.

Crucially, if we are to give up being the boss who knows and decides everything, we must have some ways of finding out what the land wants and needs. There are very many ways of doing this, some more familiar than others.

Using Our Senses

Knowing a place intimately means using all our senses to detect the smallest changes, of season, of habit, of need. It means becoming aware of when the growth of one habitat, such as a bramble thicket, is putting another, such as a wildflower meadow, out of balance. But it also means seeing how far the butterflies and birds need those same brambles for food and shelter. It means knowing when and where the buzzards are nesting and need to be left undisturbed for a while, noticing if the frogs are spawning in that boggy corner by the hedge. Essentially, it means having a sense of when to stay out of the way, and when to intervene.

Exploring Resources

In these pages we can only hint at the wealth of expertise available – biological, agricultural, environmental – to support this aim of understanding what the land needs. Many organisations provide help and advice, from the Wildlife Trusts and the RSPB to the Soil Association and the Centre for Alternative Technology, as do books, pamphlets and the internet. You'll need discrimination to judge between competing ideas and interests, and it will all come back to your own intent with the land, and your own skill in hearing its needs. (*see Useful Resources, p. A1*)

Feeling, Intuition, Meditation

Other ways to tune into and understand the land may at first seem less familiar. Our emotions give us clues about how the land and the living beings upon it are feeling.

We all remember times when we have walked on a hill or by a stream and felt joyous, as if uplifted by the energy of the place itself. There are trees we are happy to go and sit with, others that seem hidden, not to want human company. There are places where we feel fearful, or shy, times when we feel invited to explore a shady corner, and times when it seems to want us to keep out.

Living sensitively with the land, pausing to sense the energies of a place, we gradually become attuned and more able to hear, more and more open, until a walk becomes like a conversation, a series of meetings.

It can also be fun – and sometimes very important – to make imaginative journeys with the land. To do this, simply go and sit in some quiet place, by a tree that welcomes you and feels protective, or a rock that gives you a sense of being held and supported, or lie in the grasses and flowers of a meadow. Close your eyes, and ask the land beneath and around you for protection. Breathe deeply a few times, relaxing as much as you can. Now imagine yourself on a journey of discovery, flying high above the land as a bird or butterfly, or travelling deep into the earth. You might find yourself merging with the stream, or diving deep into the pond, or becoming one with the tree, feeling its roots burrowing through the earth and its branches swaying in the wind. However you do this, what matters is for you to find and trust your own way of hearing the voice of the Earth.

Truly being with the land is a process of listening and learning, of sinking, expanding into the cycles of the Earth and tuning into her voice, its vibrations so slow and deep they can pass unnoticed. Within these vast cycles, you may become aware of the lightning-fast flickerings of life, the ceaseless motion within everything.

As you sit with your eyes closed, listen, smell, feel all that is around you. Wait patiently. What is stirred in you by the breeze, how do you feel the earth, what memories open into the warmth of the sunlight? As you walk the land, read it with the soles of your feet. Expand into what comes, no matter how irrational it may seem. If prayer is your way, pray for guidance, as you quest what it means to be a guardian of this part of the Earth. There is much to be learnt in these ways, a knowledge and a seeing that is far from human, and of great assistance in this co-operative making of sanctuary.

Memories and Records

Wherever you are, stone and soil and tree hold their own memories, and gradually you may come to know something of these. Other people who lived in harmony with the land have left their memories too, in records of land-use and field-names. Some people find that, as they come to know a place where others have lived over time, they will begin to sense the memories that the land holds of them, as a kind of energetic imprint.

Other Guardians of the Earth

We are not the only beings who stand in guardianship of the land. Whether or not we are aware of them, the Earth has many guardians who are non-human. As stories and myths show, there have always been people who are aware of these other guardians of the Earth. All over the world there are traditions which tell of the 'little people', the 'tylwyth teg' of Wales, the 'fair folk' of Ireland. They have the wisdom of aeons to share with those who can come to them with respect and honouring.

If this holds meaning for you, expand your senses and feel for the earth guardians in those moments when the beauty around you touches you deeply. You may hear a call to work with these other guardians of the land, however it is that you sense them, and to learn from them another dimension of guardianship.

In coming to a particular place with the intent of guardianship, it is important to remember that there may already be others doing this, and not to assume that this is something only a human can do. Tread carefully, and listen to the land for guidance.

The Time-scale

Give it time – don't rush. In many traditions the one who is on a quest has to spend 'a year and a day' allowing the deeper meanings of experiences and teachings to emerge, and it is wise to take this period of time literally.

Give yourself and the land time to get to know each other, to learn each other's rhythms, to be with each other in all seasons. Notice how the land feels and looks at night as well as by day, in sun and wind, rain and cold. There are many clues to help you – the plants and animals on your land will show you where the land feels healthy, and where it is struggling. Put your awareness into the land, see with the senses of the plants and animals, reach out to the vast cycles of the stars and planets, of moon and sun.

With the cosmic dance comes the familiar cycle of seasons and years, the known pattern by which we measure our own ageing. In just a handful of these years, small mammals are born, grow, mate, have young, and die. We have few long-term companions, perhaps a beloved dog or cat for a decade, or a horse for a while longer.

This is one reason why we are so drawn to the trees. They alone, of all the plants and animals sharing the land with us, outlast us. We can plant them in our youth and still not see them at their greatest height and zest, so that it is possible for us to die knowing that we truly leave something growing and enduring behind us. Or we can walk amongst the old ones and ask them to speak of centuries past, of the ancestors we have never seen, but who walked amongst them, too. Those who plant trees to outlive them truly know what it means not to be attached to outcome, profit or instant gratification, but to enjoy the journey and the companionship along the way.

"A butterfly's life may last just a few days; the blossom is no sooner on the tree than it opens, fades, blows away; the berries ripen, then fall; the hazel nuts formed through winter, spring and summer are taken before they are even ripe. Through all this change the Moon holds a steady beat as she renews herself, grows to fullness, flooding the Earth with energy and light, then rises later and later as she wanes into the dark, before she begins to wax once more."

Different Types of Land

Keeping land as sanctuary can be done on any scale. A garden can become a haven for an amazing number of birds, insects, small mammals, amphibians, etc. Larger areas can be kept as unfarmed, ungrazed sanctuary, or light grazing and/or haymaking can be used in a way that benefits the variety of plants growing there. Any type of land can be treated as wildlife reserve or sanctuary.

❀ 'Improved', heavily-farmed, 'good' farmland is the most expensive to buy, and the poorest in terms of wildlife. However, planted with mixed native broadleaf trees such as oak, ash, birch, alder, etc. (for which there are grants available), and with stock-proof fencing (if surrounding land is grazed), after a few years this will support a thriving population of small birds and a gradually-increasing variety of plants.

❀ 'Poor' farmland – rough grazing, bog, steep hillside (such as valley sides), rocky ground, etc. – is cheaper to buy, and is likely to be supporting more wildlife already. It may need little management, other than cutting down on any grazing and making sure no one comes along with a bulldozer. This kind of land is probably the best for the creation of a sanctuary, as it is likely to have some trees, scrub and a variety of plants, with their birds and insects.

❀ Woodland comes in various forms. Native deciduous woodland is a wonderful habitat, needing little help, apart from protection from grazing so that the trees can regenerate. Conifer plantations are a poor habitat. For the most part they are an unnatural monoculture of tree species which are not native to these islands, so support very little of our native wildlife. (A few animals, such as polecats and foxes, do enjoy the protection offered by the dense vegetation.) However, once the conifers have been cut down (if this has already been done, the land may be sold extremely cheaply) and if the land is left alone, apart from a stock-proof fence (if needed), there will be considerable regrowth of willow and birch scrub, supporting many insects and small birds. Self-sown conifers will need to be removed, but little else needs to be done for the land to become a haven for many species.

"The silence of landscape conceals vast presence. Place is not simply location. A place is a profound individuality. Its surface texture of grass and stone is blessed by rain, wind and light."
John O'Donohue, Anam Cara

Keeping the Boundaries

Since the intent of land kept as sanctuary is usually different from that of the surrounding land, the maintenance of an effective boundary is essential.

On the physical level, whatever form the boundary takes, it must be stock-proof if you're in an area where there is livestock farming. If possible, it should be made to a high enough standard to need little time-consuming maintenance in subsequent years. A weak boundary needs constant vigilance and repair and, as the sanctuary land is likely to have much more vegetation on it than the surrounding land, it will become increasingly attractive to grazing animals. As the land becomes more 'overgrown', so the task of finding (let alone removing) stray sheep from the undergrowth becomes ever more daunting. If trees are planted, then livestock can do them a great deal of damage in a short time in their early years.

A good fence (or hedge, wall, etc., although fences are often the most effective and cheapest option) will also act as some deterrent to those who have the destruction of wildlife in mind, such as fox-hunters, salmon-poachers, or those shooting pheasants and pigeons.

On more subtle levels, the energy held by those acting as guardians of a sanctuary is very different from that of those who see the land primarily as an economic asset. The 'feel' of a sanctuary needs to be one of safety and peace, with an honouring and valuing of the sacredness of all life, and of the interconnectedness of all forms of life, including human. Energy respects boundaries only if they are held strongly by the guardians, with that intent. If this is not done, the prevailing thought-forms of exploitation of, and disregard for, the natural worlds will spread over this part of the Earth, and will have a major impact on the degree to which it can truly provide sanctuary.

In order to hold the boundaries strongly on this energetic level, it is important that they are clearly defined and marked with a physical fence or barrier that will hold the energy. Regularly 'walking the bounds' with the intent of reinforcing the boundary on all levels (as was a tradition in many parishes until quite recently) is an effective way of strengthening the boundary.

As well as strengthening boundaries, you may need to clear negative energies from the land within. A traditional way to sweep away negative energies, such as what may linger in a place once used as a dump long after the actual rubbish has been cleared from it, is to use one of the most readily available resources on most land – brambles. The long prickly stems are perfect for this work – simply cut long strands and sweep the surface of the land until it feels clear. Negative energy will be caught by the prickles, so after you have finished, it's important to burn the brambles you have used, thanking them for their help.

Outside undesirable energies can affect us through our fears and other weaknesses, so it is important for those holding the safety of part of the Earth to hold to their own truth and light, in whatever way they choose to express that. It is vital to realise that the land will be affected by whoever lives or spends time on it, by the beliefs they hold, and the integrity with which they lead their lives.

Outlay in Time, Energy & Money

Creating a sanctuary can begin on as small or large a scale as you can manage. When you assess your resources, it's important to consider your own energy now and in the future, as well as thinking about energy in the form of funds. A precise answer to the question 'How much time, energy and money is needed for the guardianship of land kept as sanctuary?' is difficult, since each piece of land is different. Much depends on what the land needs, and on what choices are made by the human guardians. However, many different kinds of land will need the following basic tasks. Some are essential, others desirable but optional, and the estimates of time required are approximate.

Essential Tasks:

Boundary fencing

If surrounding or nearby land is grazed, a good stock-proof fence is essential. Cost – approx. £2.50/metre for the initial fence, followed by occasional maintenance – a few new fence posts each year, and replacement gates when needed, plus labour. Time – regular checking and maintenance takes a few days a year, depending on the size of the land (and the athleticism and determination of the local sheep). A boundary fence is likely to need replacing every twenty to thirty years.

Weed control round newly-planted trees

This helps the trees to grow faster – without it they may get suffocated in undergrowth. It can be achieved by spraying, but in a sanctuary this option is not likely to be chosen. A combination of hand-weeding and mulching (mulch mats or old carpet are best) works well. Time – for a few acres of young trees, several days a year for the first few years.

Thinning of young trees

After eight to ten years, if thinning is not done, there is a danger of the trees getting drawn up and then windblown. Time – a few days' work with a chainsaw (or longer by hand) in winter, every two to three years, plus more work to extract the wood for firewood, if so desired – and if possible. Dead wood may be left to lie, as it is an extremely valuable resource for fungi, wood-boring insects, woodpeckers and other birds, etc. Woodlands, parks or gardens that are kept too 'tidy' lack this important part of woodland ecology.

Clearing ditches

Needed where flooding would, for example, damage access tracks or interfere with the water supply for a pond. Time – a couple of days' work with a hired mini-digger, every few years.

Listening to the land

A vital way to come to know what is needed, so that you are able to make the choices about management which feel right for this particular place and time. Costs nothing, can be done in any time available, day or night – one of the rewards of living with land that you love.

Desirable, Optional Tasks

These examples all help to maintain valuable wildlife habitats on the land where these are becoming less common elsewhere.

Making hay off an unimproved meadow, so that the variety of wildflowers is maintained. The value of the hay should more than cover the cost of paying contractors/neighbours to cut and bale it.

Clearing scrub from bog land to favour the plants and insects which live in the bog. Labour intensive, unless done by light grazing.

Clearing brambles from areas where other plants, such as flowers needed by butterflies and moths, can then grow. Labour intensive, and also repetitive – needs doing every year.

Hedge laying and/or trimming – prolongs the life of the hedge, and improves it as a habitat for small birds, mammals, etc. Best done every few years, but costly in labour.

Internal fencing – may be needed if the land is grazed at all.

Nest-boxes for birds and bats – putting up and maintaining these will take a few days' work each winter.

Keeping Animals

There is an ancient harmony between the land and animals, and there was a time when people helped to hold that balance. But in the past few hundred years we have selectively bred domestic animals in a way which has increasingly distorted and upset this relationship.

Making the decision to hold land as a sanctuary offers an opportunity to enter into a different relationship with those animals which have been exploited, and used by us to exploit the land. This has been fostered by the subsidy system, which has set maximum numbers for sheep and cattle per acre/hectare, and concentrates subsidies on young animals. The results are overgrazing and reliance on chemicals, both as fertilisers and pesticides, and for treating animals in order to keep the system functioning. And it is rare these days to see elderly animals because of the practice of routinely destroying animals which are more than a few years old.

For at least the last few hundred years our landscape has been a farmed one. Traditional farming methods allowed a great variety of wild animals, plants, insects, birds to flourish alongside the domestic sheep, cattle, pigs, horses and crops. So when we think of conservation of the species that are fast disappearing (such as the skylark, or lapwing), we are often looking at helping to preserve those species which have learned to co-exist with farming.

What this means in terms of sanctuary is that we are looking at choices – whatever we decide about the management of the land will affect what kinds of life it supports now and in the future. For example, if we want to help orchids to survive in an area of grazing land, it is important that the right level of grazing is continued, by the appropriate kinds of animals, at the most helpful times of year. Animals do have a major impact on the land, but this can be harnessed in particular ways, e.g. to reduce reed growth, to control brambles or bracken, to create the best conditions for flowering plants and butterflies to survive on pastureland. Equally, young trees and hedges need protection from grazing animals.

Since every piece of land is different, it's not possible to be specific, but a realistic management plan can be worked out through a combination of gathering available advice with trial and error. If the sanctuary land has been extensively grazed, then any dramatic change in management is likely to result in other dramatic changes, like the loss of some flower species which flourish in short grasses. It would be wise to take time to walk your land, with the intent of discovering everything that is growing there, before deciding, for example, what needs to be supported with grazing by which animals, and when.

Once again, listen to the land and the animals, and be prepared to be flexible. Animals, whether wild or domestic, bond very strongly with land, and it is important not to get into conflict with them. Some land is crossed by ancient animal trackways, of badger, fox and deer, for example. The free movement of these animals is part of the song of the land. It is recognised by domestic animals, and needs to be respected within any management system.

If you want to keep domestic animals in a sanctuary, you will need to honour their needs, attending to their health and welfare. Just like wild animals, sheep and cows have their own natural rhythms, their times of rest and growing, their favourite places on the land, their own particular trackways from one place to another, their individual personalities and their complex social organisations. They form strong relationships with one another, both bonds and rivalries. It is important to have ways to catch up animals without stirring up wild or panicky energy in the sanctuary. A system where the animals can move at their own natural pace from larger to smaller areas, or pens, generally works well, while electric fencing and netting can be a useful way of moving animals around the land and protecting areas without erecting permanent fencing.

Animals should be cared for organically, wherever possible, both for their own well-being and for that of the land and watercourses. Organic animal feed is available, and there are gentle, balanced ways of keeping animals healthy, such as herbal and homeopathic treatment. There are now a number of vets with a knowledge of homeopathy, and the Soil Association (see *Useful Resources*, p. A6) can supply lists of medicines and treatments which are acceptable within an organic system.

Animals naturally mate and breed – sheep certainly will go to extraordinary lengths to do so! Their numbers will expand, since there are no significant natural predators, so you will need to decide what to do about this. You will also have to consider reducing their numbers if the land and the animals do not thrive together naturally and harmoniously. Deciding whether animals are killed for meat must be left up to the individual conscience. Many people feel that this is acceptable if the animals have been humanely reared and humanely slaughtered.

If your animals are not being reared for meat, you will need to think about other ways of keeping their numbers manageable. You might decide to keep rare breeds, in which case there are a number of organisations and magazines where you can advertise stock for sale (such as the Rare Breeds Survival Trust, see *Useful Resources*, p. A5). This is also a way to help preserve the old breeds.

The key to keeping animals on a part of the Earth held as sanctuary is to keep only as many animals as you can know and love individually, and only as many as will allow both them and the land to thrive. In this way there will be enough for all to share.

The Garden

Exactly the same principles apply when creating a garden sanctuary as with farmland. Start with what is already there – what does it tell you? Don't be too hasty to clear away piles of rotting wood, or to wield the chainsaw. Take time just to be with the land, to see what happens there through the seasons. What 'weeds' take root in your garden, what beetles push through the grass, what butterflies sun themselves on the leaves?

It is about finding the 'flow' of your particular piece of land, getting to know its rhythms, what plants flourish there, noticing where the sunlight falls at different times of the year, how the moon and stars look in summer and winter, when are its times of flood or drought – and noticing, too, any persistent problems. Everything you see and hear, feel and smell, will tell you more about living with this piece of land. Keep a diary of your garden, take photos – immerse yourself in its life.

"Beauty is in the rhythms of shape and line, of the way the shadows are held in the cool dankness within the stone walls, of how the sing of the stars is received within the branches of the hawthorn, the volume of space where the sunlight falls. It is in the ferns and ivy, the spider-webs spanning the path, the holly seedlings that have come for the first time this year. It is in the tiny pale green eggs of the shield-bugs and their heraldic adult selves, in the unbelievable fire of the holly blue butterfly dancing over the leaves, even in the magnificence of the slugs, prehistoric in their imperturbable focus on existence . . ."

Local Provenance

Whether we are planting trees, hedges, crops or garden plants, what's known as 'local provenance' is vitally important. We've learned that planting non-native varieties of tree or shrub can damage an ecosystem, but ensuring that we plant only native oaks or hawthorns, for example, is still not enough. It's become clear that to maintain and reclaim the vitality of a piece of land what we plant there must be of 'local provenance', grown from local varieties. This applies to hedges on farmland as much as to garden sanctuaries – if we don't do this, we are doing far less than we intend to help the ecosystem we care so much about. In fact, we are actually causing harm in the long term, as non-native varieties hybridise with the native stock, and the synchronised time-cycles of plant and animal are thrown out of step.

Every habitat has evolved its own delicately-balanced sequences to suit soil and climate and geography. For example, tender new leaves unfold on an oak tree in spring just as millions of insect larvae emerge to eat them. The gorging caterpillars then provide vital protein for newly hatched blue-tit chicks. Timing is everything in the life-cycles of plant, bird, insect, mammal, all connected to the cycles of the seasons and weather. A plant will flower at the time when its main pollinators are abundant, to ensure that it sets as much seed as possible. When we unwittingly plant an eastern-European variety of primrose – supplied by the huge commercial nurseries because they find it easier to propagate and more hardy than our native variety of the same species, ignoring the fact that it flowers a few days later or earlier – we are tearing a hole in the complex web of life.

Of course, this is a problem which goes beyond 'private' planting. An oak-tree from Berkshire may be botanically identical to one from the South Wales Valleys, but it has evolved in a different climate, on different soil and at a different altitude.

Use it in 'greening' derelict industrial land in the Valleys and, while it may seem to 'fit', supporting plenty of predators and pollinators, it is a short-term fix. Planting in this way does not restore the habitat. Year by year there are fewer insects, fewer birds, a diminished diversity of species. Meanwhile, what remains of the local habitat is under threat, eaten away by building development.

You are unlikely to be in charge of public planting, and you may have only a small piece of land in your guardianship, but anything you can do to restore the local habitat will have an effect beyond the sanctuary within your garden walls.

Public Land

Many of us live in cities, and may not have even a small garden. But there is no reason why we shouldn't still hear the call of the Earth and respond by doing what we can to create places of sanctuary.

The first step is to look for a place on the land where you can hear the cry of the land, where you are touched by the beauty all around you. This can happen even in the midst of urban decay and dereliction. When you have found such a place, offer yourself to the land as a guardian, and listen for a response. Be open to what comes, and trust your perceptions. Every guardian has duties – yours might be as simple and obvious as picking up litter, or you could be asked to plant trees, make a boundary, sing songs or tell stories, or simply to sit still and be with the land.

Whatever you feel called to do as a guardian, coming to know the true nature of the relationship between the land and the human is a joyful experience, whether or not the land is 'yours'. As you bring your vision to the place which sings to you, by as simple an action as removing litter, so you are giving other people the opportunity to see this part of the Earth in a different way.

A Spiritual Relationship

Sanctuary is a state of mind – it is to hold a place and the life in it sacred, and to take on the responsibilities of a guardian to that place. In each of us there is a memory of this way of being with the land – at heart, we know how to restore and re-create the sacred relationship between us and the land. And all the help we need is available, whether from other humans or from the land itself.

Sanctuary starts in the heart. It is a dynamic living interchange between us and the Earth which is our home. It is a state of being, an awareness in every moment of our place in the web of life. Instead of managing the land to human ends, the guardian comes to the land in a way of co-creation, seeking to learn from the land how best to be with it. We hold the Earth in trust for our children and for their children to come. There is nothing airy-fairy about guardianship – it has to be down to earth, in every sense. It is not a denial of the human, but a celebration of human and land together.

Sanctuary is an inner feeling, the knowing of a golden space of wholeness and harmony, a place within each of us where the soul feels nurtured. A single blade of grass can evoke this inner refuge, can satisfy the thirst of the spirit. And so a place of sanctuary, a moment of touching the infinite in woodland or mountain-top, seashore or desert, is recognised by that inner place. It possesses wholeness and harmony, life flows there unbroken between all that is: tree and moss and earth, sky and stone and stream, cloud and wind and light, and the moving beings, the birds and insects we see and those larger ones who move unseen – and, if we are to be more than observer, we, the humans, must enter this unbroken stream and flow with all.

When you find the point of harmony, everything falls into place. The striving falls away, and there is a sense of simplicity. It is like having an effortless, joyful conversation, giving for the sheer joy of giving, reflecting the beauty of life back to the Earth and so completing the circle. And that feeling of harmony will help to sustain you through all the setbacks and back-breaking physical effort, to find a wider and deeper vision in rain, wind and drought.

Useful Resources

Further Reading - Books

Anam Cara, Eternal Echoes*
John O'Donohue; Bantam Books; 1999, 2000

BTCV Handbooks:* dry-stone walling, tree planting, hedging, etc.
Excellent practical conservation handbooks; BTCV Enterprises

Escape from the Rat Race:* downshifting to a richer life
Nicholas Corder; Elliot Right Way Books; 2001.

Gaia:* the practical science of planetary medicine
James Lovelock; Gaia Books; 1995

The Little Earth Book *
James Bruges; Alistair Sawday; 2000

The Living Land *
Jules Pretty; Earthscan; 1999

Practical Rare Breeds
Valerie Porter; Pelham Books; 1987

Self Reliance:* a recipe for the new millennium
John Yeoman; Permanent Publications; 2000

The Whole House Book:* ecological building design and materials
Pat Borer and Cindy Harris; CAT Publications; 1998

Tree Wisdom:* guide to the myth, folklore and healing power of trees
Jacqueline Memory Paterson; Thorsons; 1996

*Titles marked * are available from Permaculture Magazine's Earth Repair Catalogue along with around 500 other titles. For your free copy please contact:*
Permanent Publications, The Sustainability Centre, East Meon, Hampshire, GU32 1HR, UK. Tel: 0845 458 4150 (UK only) or 01730 823 311 Fax: 01730 823 322
Email: orders@permaculture.co.uk Web: www.permaculture.co.uk

Further Reading - Magazines UK

The Ark: magazine of the Rare Breeds Survival Trust. Quarterly. Tel: 024 7669 6551 Fax: 024 7669 6706 Web: www.rbst.org.uk

Clean Slate: the latest news of alternative and sustainable technologies. Quarterly. Centre for Alternative Technology (CAT). Tel: 01654 705 959 Web: www.cat.org.uk

Country Smallholding: about organic smallholding. Monthly. Buriton Hse, Station Rd, Newport, Saffron Walden, Essex CB11 3PL. Tel: 01799 540 922 Web: www.countrysmallholding.com

The Ecologist: examining today's environmental, social and political models. Monthly. Unit 18, Chelsea Wharf, London SW10 0QJ. Tel: 020 7351 3578 Fax: 020 7351 3617 Web: www.theecologist.org

Living Earth: campaigning for organic food and farming and sustainable forestry. Quarterly. Soil Association. Tel: 0117 929 0661 Fax: 0117 925 2504 Web: www.soilassociation.org

Permaculture Magazine: solutions for sustainable living. The No.1 sustainable lifestyle magazine. Quarterly. Permanent Publications. Tel: 01730 823 311 Fax: 01730 823 322 Web: www.permaculture.co.uk

Resurgence: an international forum for ecological and spiritual thinking. Bi-monthly. Ford House, Hartland, Bideford, Devon EX39 6EE. Tel: 01208 841 824 Web: www.resurgence.org

Smallholder: magazine for smallholders, includes information on organics. Monthly. 3 Falmouth Business Park, Bickland Water Road, Falmouth, Cornwall. Tel: 01326 213 333 Fax: 01326 212 108

Tree News: the magazine of the Tree Council, an umbrella group linking major tree organisations in the UK. 51 St Catherine Place, London SW1E 6DY. Tel: 020 7828 9928 Web: www.treecouncil.org.uk

Further Reading - Magazines Ireland

Aisling magazine: An Charraig, Mainistir, Inis Mor, Aran Islands, County Galway. Tel/Fax: 099 61245 Web: www. aislingmagazine.com

Source magazine: 166 Lower Rathmines Rd, Dublin 6. Tel: 01 491 1711 Fax: 01 491 1710 Web: www.youaresource.com

Wild Ireland magazine: wildlife and environmental issues. Leinster Mills, Naas, Co Kildare. Tel: 045 894 900 Fax: 045 894 905 Web: www.wildireland.ie

Network Ireland: Ballydonahane, Bodyke, Co Clare. Tel/Fax: 061 921 642

EarthWatch: the magazine of Friends of the Earth Ireland. c/o Lothar Lucan, Dromore, Bantry, Co Cork. Tel: 028 31853

Organic Matters: journal of the Irish Organic Farmers' and Growers' Association. Bi-monthly. 27 Kilcross Court, Sandyford, Dublin 18. Tel: 01 294 3459 Web: www.organicmattersmag.com

Organisations - UK

Bat Conservation Trust: umbrella organisation for local bat groups. 15 Cloisters House, 8 Battersea Park Road, London SW8 4BG. Tel: 020 7627 2629 Fax: 020 7627 2628 Web: www.bats.org

British Dragonfly Society: Secretary: Dr W H Wain, The Haywain, Hollywater Road, Bordon, Hampshire GU35 0AD. Web: www.dragonflysoc.org.uk

British Herpetological Society: c/o The Zoological Society of London, Regent's Park, London NW1 4RY.

BTCV (British Trust For Conservation Volunteers): 36 St Mary's Street, Wallingford, Oxfordshire OX10 0EU. Tel: 01491 821 600 Web: www.btcv.org

Organisations - UK continued

British Trust for Ornithology (BTO): The Nunnery, Thetford, Norfolk IP24 2PU. Tel: 01842 750 050 Fax: 10842 750 030 Web: www.bto.org

Butterfly Conservation: Manor Yard, East Lulworth, Wareham, Dorset BH20 5QP. Tel: 01929 400 209 Web: www.butterfly-conservation.org

Centre for Alternative Technology (CAT): Machynlleth, Powys SY20 9AZ. Tel: 01654 705 959 Web: www.cat.org.uk

Countryside Council for Wales/Cyngor Cefn Gwlad Cymru: gives grants for traditional forms of conservation under the Tir Gofal scheme. Plas Penrhos, Ffordd Penrhos, Bangor, Gwynedd LL57 2LQ. Tel: 01248 385 500 Fax: 01248 355 782 Web: www.ccw.gov.uk

Flora Locale: information about 'local provenance', details of suppliers of native plants. Web: www.floralocale.org

Forestry Commission: advice, information, grants. 231 Corstorphine Road, Edinburgh EH12 7AT. Tel: 0131 334 0303 Fax: 0131 334 4472 Web: www.forestry.gov.uk

Friends of the Earth: 26-28 Underwood Street, London N1 7JQ. Tel: 020 7490 1555 Fax: 020 7490 0881 Web: www.foe.co.uk

Froglife: Mansion House, 27-28 Market Place, Halesworth, Suffolk IP19 8AY. Tel: 01986 873 733 Fax: 01986 874 744 Web: www.froglife.org

FWAG (Farming and Wildlife Advisory Group): National Agricultural Centre, Stoneleigh, Kenilworth, Warwickshire CV8 2RX. Tel: 02476 696 699 Fax: 02476 696 760 Web: www.fwag.org.uk

Henry Doubleday Research Association (HDRA): Ryton Organic Gardens, Coventry CV8 3LG. Tel: 02476 303 517 Fax: 02476 639 229 Web: www.hdra.org.uk

Herpetological Conservation Trust: 655a Christchurch Road, Boscombe, Bournemouth BH1 4AP. Tel: 01202 391 319
Web: www.HerpConsTrust.org.uk

Land Heritage Trust: charity which owns and lets farmland to be farmed organically. Pound Corner, Whitestone, Exeter, Devon EX4 2HP. Tel: 01647 61099 Fax: 01647 61134 Web: www.landheritage.org

Mammal Society: 15 Cloisters House, 8 Battersea Park Road, London SW8 4BG. Tel: 020 7498 4358 Web: www.abdn.ac.uk/mammal

Organic Centre Wales/Canolfan Organig Cymru: Institute of Rural Studies, University of Wales, Aberystwyth, Ceredigion SY23 3AL. Tel: 01970 622 248 Fax: 01970 622 238 Web: www.organic.aber.ac.uk

Organic Gardening Catalogue: Riverdene Business Park, Molesey Road, Hersham, Surrey KT12 4RG. Tel: 01932 253 666 Fax: 01932 252 707 Web: www.organiccatalog.com

Permaculture Association (Britain): BCM Permaculture Association, London WC1N 3XX. Tel/Fax: 0845 458 1805 or 0113 262 1718
Web: www.permaculture.org.uk

Plantlife: 21 Elizabeth Street, London SW1W 9RP or c/o Natural History Museum, Cromwell Rd, London SW7 5BD.
Tel: 020 7808 0100 Fax: 020 7730 8377 Web: www.plantlife.org.uk

Rare Breeds Survival Trust (RBST): supports and promotes the conservation of rare breeds of farm animals. National Agricultural Centre, Stoneleigh Park, Warwickshire CV8 2LG.
Tel: 024 7669 6551 Fax: 024 7669 6706 Web: www.rbst.org.uk

Royal Society for the Protection of Birds (RSPB): The Lodge, Sandy, Bedfordshire SG19 2DL. Tel: 01767 680 551 Web: www.rspb.org.uk

Organisations - UK continued

Schumacher College: an international centre for ecological studies. The Old Postern, Dartington, Totnes, Devon TQ9 6EA. Tel: 01803 865 934 Fax: 01803 866 899 Web: www.gn.apc.org/schumachercollege

Shared Earth Trust: runs courses in restoring biodiversity to intensively-managed farmland. Denmark Farm Conservation Centre, Betws Bledrws, Lampeter, Ceredigion SA48 8PB. Tel: 01570 493 358 Email: set@denmark-farm.freeserve.co.uk

Small Wood Association: The Old Bakery, Pontesbury, Shropshire. ST5 RR. Tel: 01743 792 644 Web: www.smallwoods.org.uk

Soil Association: Bristol House, 40-56 Victoria Street, Bristol BS1 6BY. Tel: 0117 929 0661 Fax: 0117 925 2504 Web: www.soilassociation.org

Vincent Wildlife Trust: conservation of British mammals. 3-4 Bronsil Courtyard, Eastnor, Ledbury, Herefordshire HR8 1EP. Tel: 01531 636 441 Fax: 01531 636 442 Web: www.vwt.org.uk

Wildlife Trusts: contact details for all Wildlife Trusts in the UK. Web: www.wildlifetrusts.org

Royal Society for Nature Conservation (RSNC): co-ordinates activities of Wildlife Trusts. The Kiln, Waterside, Mather Road, Newark, Nottinghamshire. NG24 1WT.
Tel: 01636 670 000 Fax: 01636 670 001 Web: www.rsnc.org

Woodland Improvement and Conservation Ltd: trees for forestry on all scales, publishes very informative handbook on forestry. Newent Lane, Huntley, Royal Forest of Dean, Gloucestershire, GL19 3HG. Tel: 01452 830 344 Web: www.woodland-improvement.co.uk

Woodland Trust: Autumn Park, Grantham, Linconshire NG31 6LL. Tel: 01476 581 111 Fax: 01476 590 808 Web: www.woodland-trust.org.uk

Organisations - Ireland

Friends of the Earth Ireland: 7 Upper Camden Street, Dublin 2. Tel: 01 497 3773 Web: www.iol.ie/~foeeire

Friends of the Irish Environment: Allihies, Co Cork. Tel: 027 73025 Web: www.anu.ie/wirl/friends

Irish Peatland Conservation Council: 119 Capel Street, Dublin 1. Tel: 01 872 2397 Web: www.ipcc.ie

Irish Wildlife Trust: 107 Lower Baggot Street, Dublin 2. Tel: 01 676 8588 Web: www.iwt.ie

Building Societies and Banks

Ecology Building Society: 18 Station Road, Cross Hills, Keithley, W. Yorks BD20 7EH. Tel: 0845 674 5566 Web: www.ecology.co.uk

Triodos Bank: NV Brunel House, 11 The Promenade, Bristol BS8 3NN. Tel: 0845 769 7239 Fax: 0117 973 9303 Web: www.triodos.co.uk

Kath Simmonds (author)

Is happy to answer enquiries about her experiences of turning an area of pastureland into a wildlife haven, as she describes in this book. Visits by appointment only. Hafodlas, Tregaron, Ceredigion SY25 6UG. Tel: 01974 298 920 Fax: 01974 299 041

TIPI LIVING

a Simple Living Series book
by Patrick Whitefield
Illustrations by
Anne Monger

Permaculture teacher, Patrick Whitefield lived in a self built tipi in Somerset for eight years. First self-published and now newly revised and updated, this is his guide to all aspects of tipi living: the story of how he came to live this way; how to choose and pitch a tipi; living with Sun and Storm; maintenance; moving; firemaking; furnishing; food and cooking in a tipi. Full of first hand experience and practical information, it is also Patrick's personal account of a time of simplicity and spiritual connection with the Earth. A delightful book for everyone interested in tipis, low impact dwelling and those who want to celebrate the simple life.

Permanent Publications; ISBN 1 85623 016 3; A5; Paperback; 48pp; 35 line drawings; Code TL1; £6.95 + p&p

PERMANENT PUBLICATIONS
The Sustainability Centre, East Meon
Hampshire GU32 1HR, UK
Tel: 0845 458 4150 or 01730 823 311
Fax: 01730 823 322
Email: orders@permaculture.co.uk

Distributed in the U.S.A. by Chelsea Green Publishing Company